SCHOLASTIC Phonics

Beachcombing

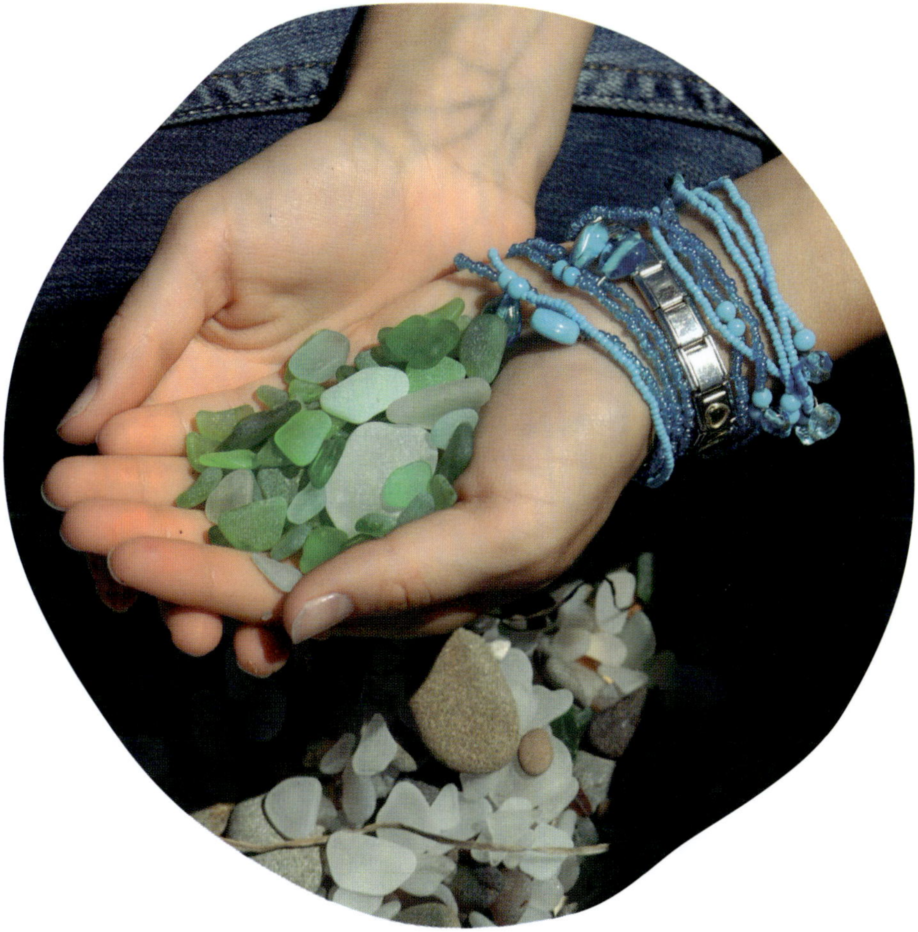

Published in the UK by Scholastic Education, 2023
Scholastic Distribution Centre, Bosworth Avenue, Tournament Fields, Warwick, CV34 6UQ
Scholastic Ireland, 89E Lagan Road, Dublin Industrial Estate, Glasnevin, Dublin, D11 HP5F

SCHOLASTIC and associated logos are trademarks and/or registered trademarks of Scholastic Inc.
www.scholastic.co.uk
© 2023 Scholastic
1 2 3 4 5 6 7 8 9   3 4 5 6 7 8 9 0 1 2

Printed by Ashford Colour Press
The book is made of materials from well-managed, FSC®-certified forests and other controlled sources.

A CIP catalogue record for this book is available from the British Library.
ISBN 978-0702-32117-7

All rights reserved. This book is sold subject to the condition that it shall not, by way of trade or otherwise, be lent, hired out or otherwise circulated in any form of binding or cover other than that in which it is published. No part of this publication may be reproduced, stored in a retrieval system, or transmitted in any form or by any other means (electronic, mechanical, photocopying, recording or otherwise) without prior written permission of Scholastic.

Every effort has been made to trace copyright holders for the works reproduced in this publication, and the publishers apologise for any inadvertent omissions.

Author
Giles Clare
Editorial team
Rachel Morgan, Vicki Yates, Gemma Smith, Jennie Clifford
Design team
Dipa Mistry, Andrea Lewis, We Are Grace
Illustrations
Bethany Lord/Advocate Art
Photographs
Cover MelanieMaya/iStock
p4 Debbie Galbraith/iStock
p1, 5 rjgrant/iStock
p8 (sun lotion) caimacanul/Shutterstock, (coat) Andrienko Anastasiya/Shutterstock, (hat) nopparada samrhubsuk/Shutterstock, (litter picker) Quang Ho/Shutterstock, (wellington boots) Nataliia K/Shutterstock
p9 (camera phone) Rsplaneta/Shutterstock, (hand gel) Suhail Suri/Shutterstock, (bag for rubbish) Olha Khomenko/Shutterstock, (drink) Lalandrew/Shutterstock, (magnifying glass) Vitaly Korovin/Shutterstock, (rucksack) Mega Pixel/Shutterstock, (box for finds) Krasyuk/iStock
p3, 10 Marieke Peche/iStock
p11 Thomas Faull/iStock
p12 abzee/iStock
p13 omgimages/iStock
p14–15 Charlesy/Shutterstock
p15 danibeder/iStock
p16 (skate fish egg sack) Noel V. Baebler/Shutterstock, (seashell) malerapaso/iStock, (fish bone) antpkr/Shutterstock
p17 (driftwood) Khomkrit art/Shutterstock, (seaweed) juniorbeep/iStock, (jellyfish) Rudimencial/iStock, (sea urchin shell) heikeinnz/iStock
p17, 19 (lightbulb) VectorCookies/iStock
p18 (sea glass) lisinski/iStock, (old coin) apalm/Shutterstock, (broken pottery) imschowe/iStock, (large pieces of netting) Aigars Reinholds/Shutterstock
p19 (fishing net float) robotrecorder/Shutterstock, (broken plastic toy) Mmassel/iStock, (crushed can) Nor Gal/Shutterstock, (dirty bottle) DeawSS/Shutterstock
p20, 24 Angelafoto/iStock
p21 Jorge Moro/iStock
p22, 24 Maria_Usp/Shutterstock
p23, 24 Neustockimages/iStock

Help your child to read!

This book practises these letters and letter sounds.
Point and say the sounds with your child:

- ey (as in 'they')
- ea (as in 'great')
- mb (as in 'comb')
- ti (as in 'action')
- ci (as in 'special')
- augh (as in 'caught')
- ore (as in 'shore')

Your child may need help to read these common tricky words:

- to
- do
- the
- of
- beautiful
- are
- against
- any
- everyone
- one
- people
- their
- many
- pretty
- move
- into
- our

Before reading
- Look at the cover picture and read the title together. Read the back cover blurb to your child.
- Ask your child: *What sort of things do you think you might find on a walk on a beach?*
- Talk about the image in the magnifying glass.

During reading
- If your child gets stuck on a word, remind them to sound it out and then blend the sounds to read the word: p-r-o-t-e-c-ti-o-n, protection.
- If they are still stuck, show them how to read the word.
- Enjoy looking at the pictures together. Pause to talk about the information.

After reading
- Talk about the images on page 24. What can your child tell you about them?
- Ask your child: *What are tides? What clothes should you wear when you go beachcombing?*
- Talk with your child about the most interesting thing they found out in the book. What was so interesting about it?

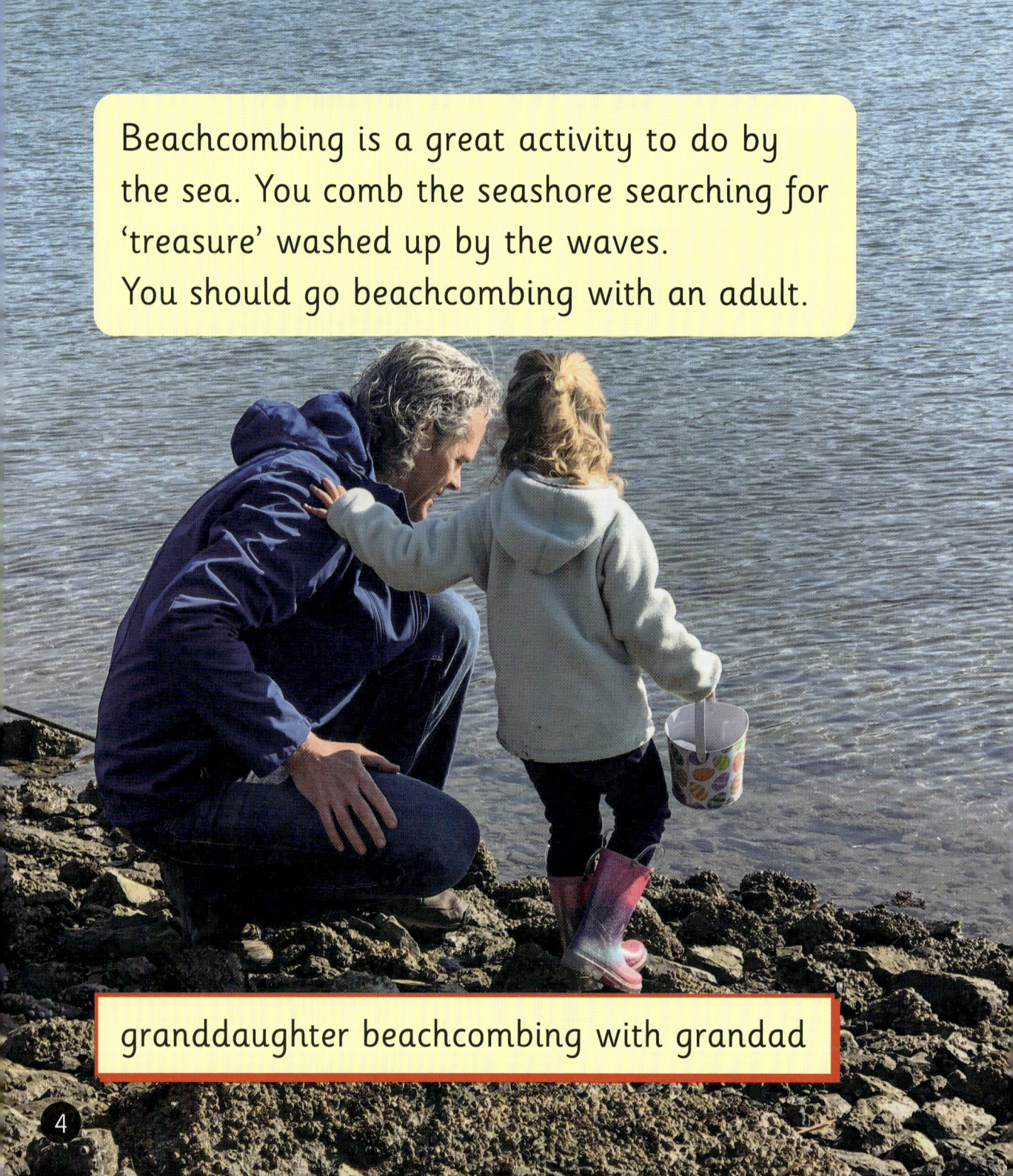

Beachcombing is a great activity to do by the sea. You comb the seashore searching for 'treasure' washed up by the waves.
You should go beachcombing with an adult.

granddaughter beachcombing with grandad

This girl has a collection of beautiful sea glass. Sea glass is broken glass that has been tumbled smooth by the sea.

You should prepare before you go beachcombing. Look at the weather forecast. Check the tides (when the sea is coming in and going out).

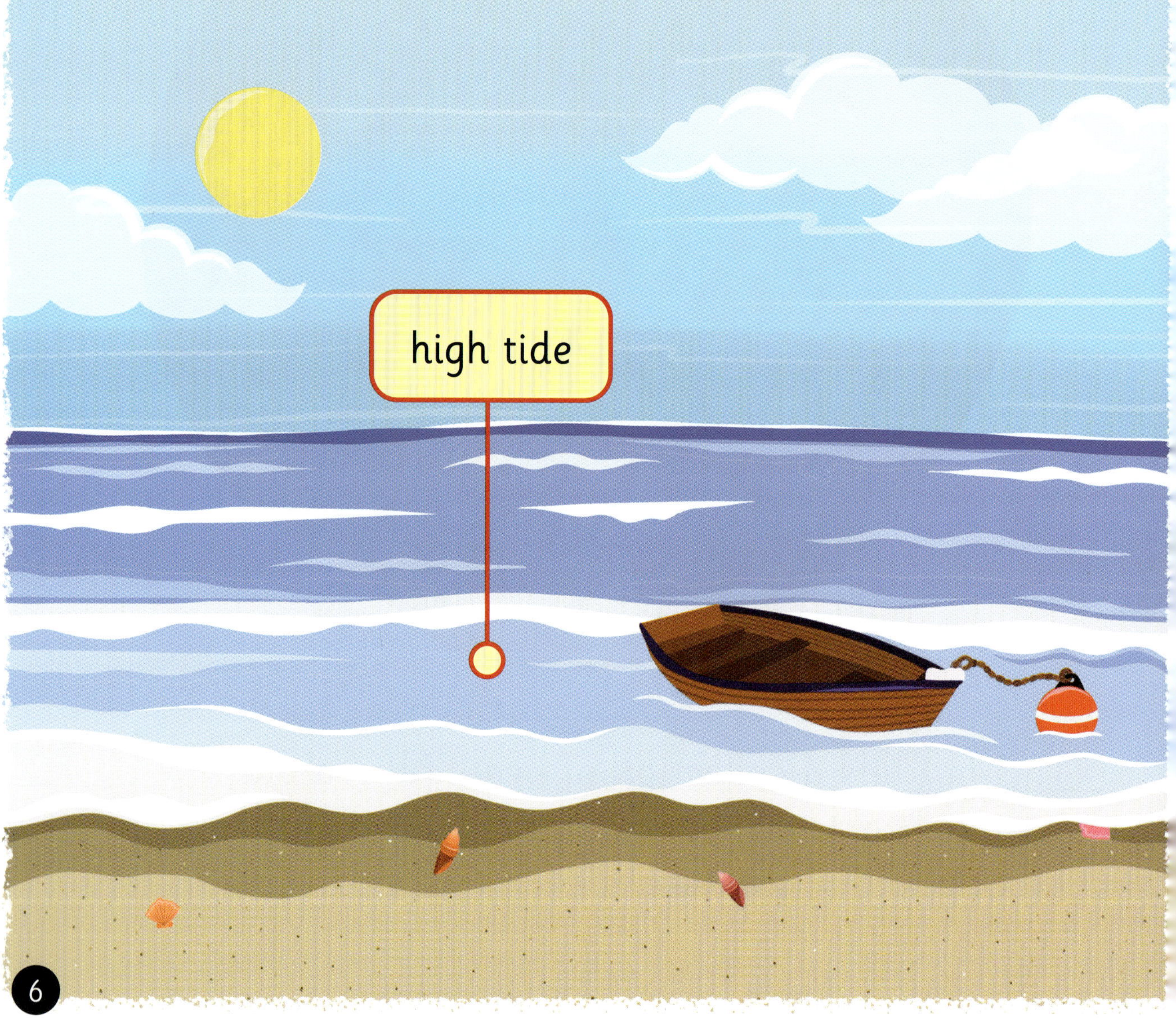

high tide

Don't get caught out by the tide. Find out the times of high tide and low tide. Start beachcombing after high tide, as the sea is going out.

low tide

Take the right clothes and equipment for exploring and for your protection. Take a box to store your special finds in (see 'Rules for Beachcombing' on page 20).

sun lotion

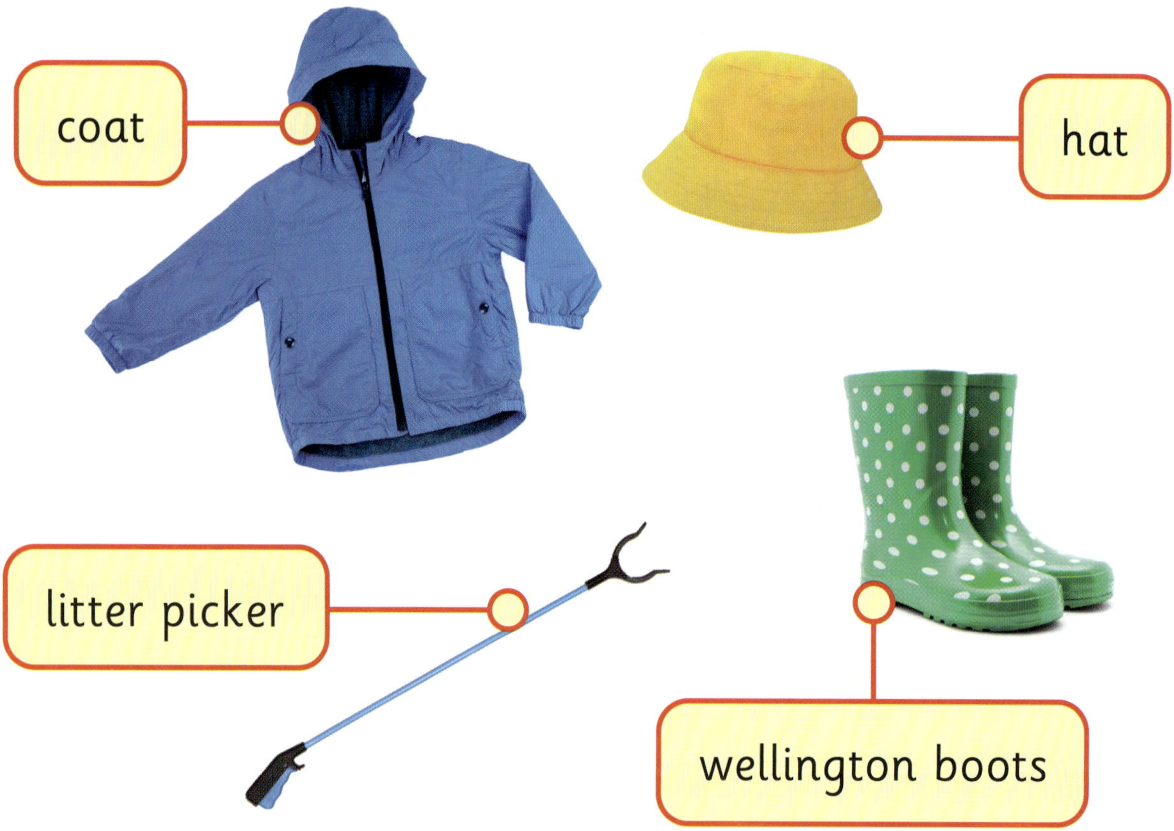

coat

hat

litter picker

wellington boots

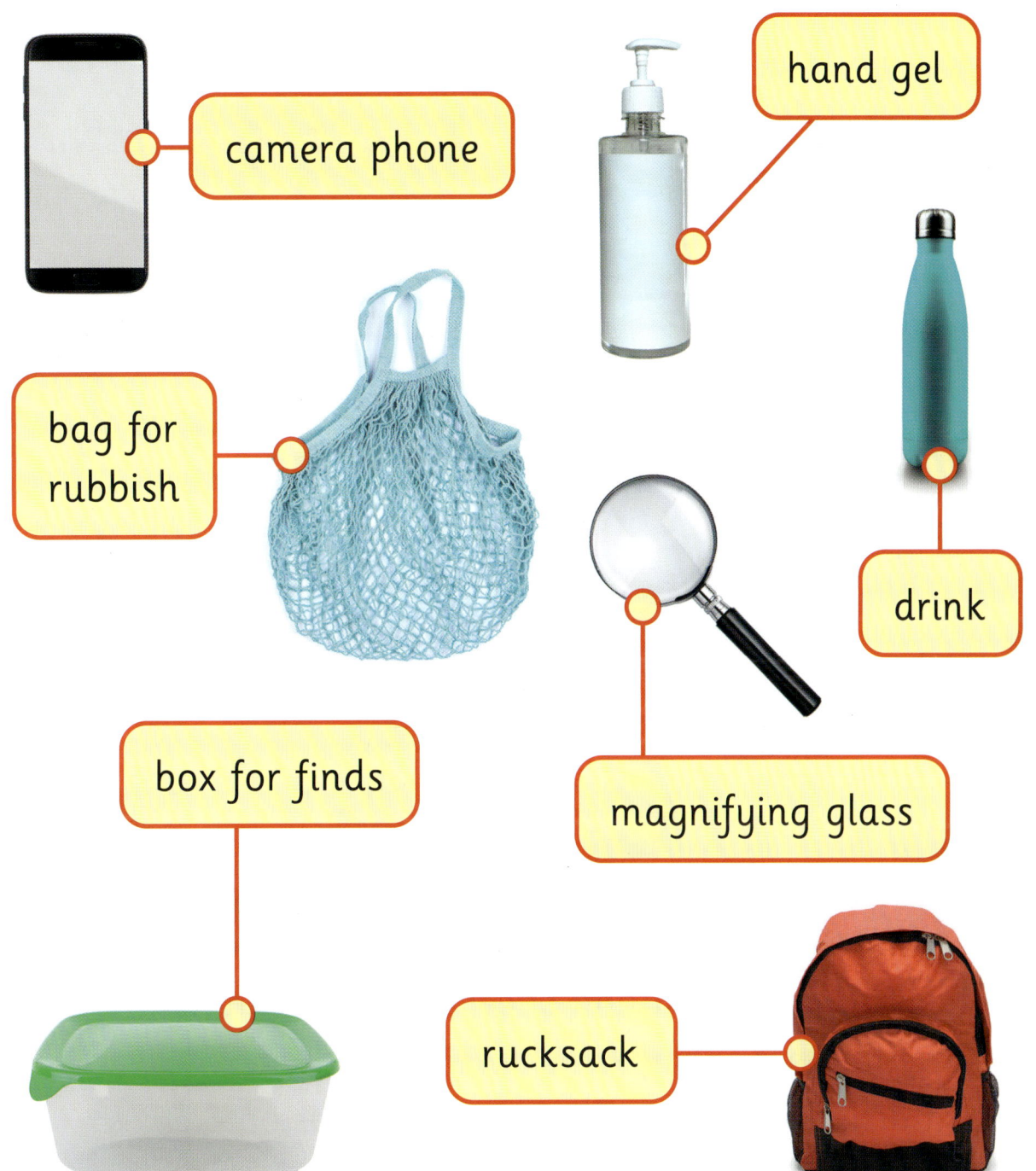

These cliffs are tall and sheer. The sea can surge against them, which weakens them and dislodges rocks. This is called erosion.

At the beach, read any signs.
Loose rocks on the face of the cliff can break away and fall onto the beach. Everyone should be taught to stay away from cliffs when beachcombing.

One of the best times to go beachcombing is after a storm. The ferocious waves can wash up strange and unusual treasures.

The storm has passed, but the weather conditions are still windy and grey. It's time for action. What mystery objects might you find?

A great place to look for beach treasure is the strandline. This is where the high tide reaches on the shoreline and objects get caught on the beach.

strandline

plastic straw

The high tide leaves lots of things on the shore. It can leave things from nature and made by people.

Here are some things from nature you might find.

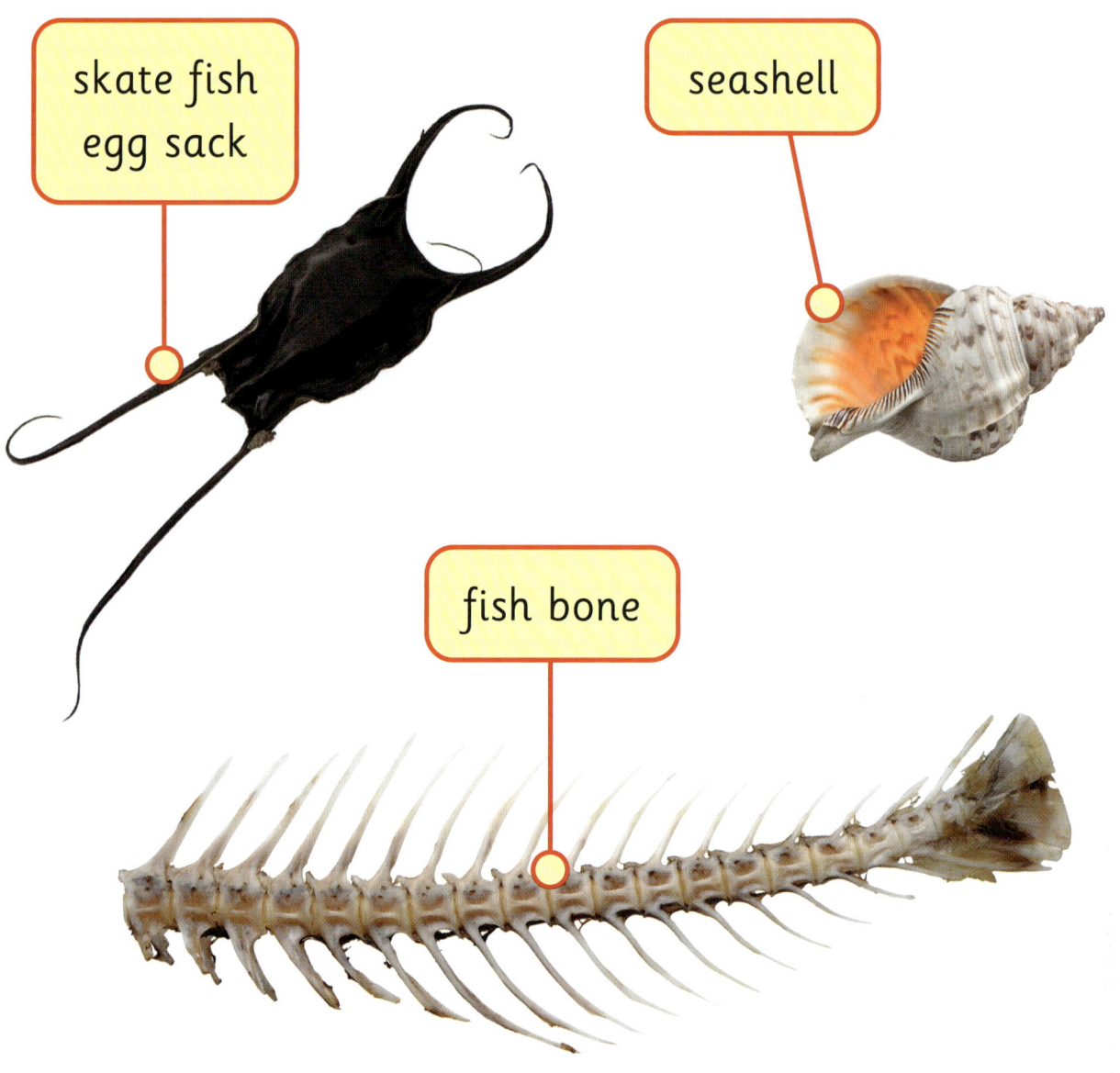

skate fish egg sack

seashell

fish bone

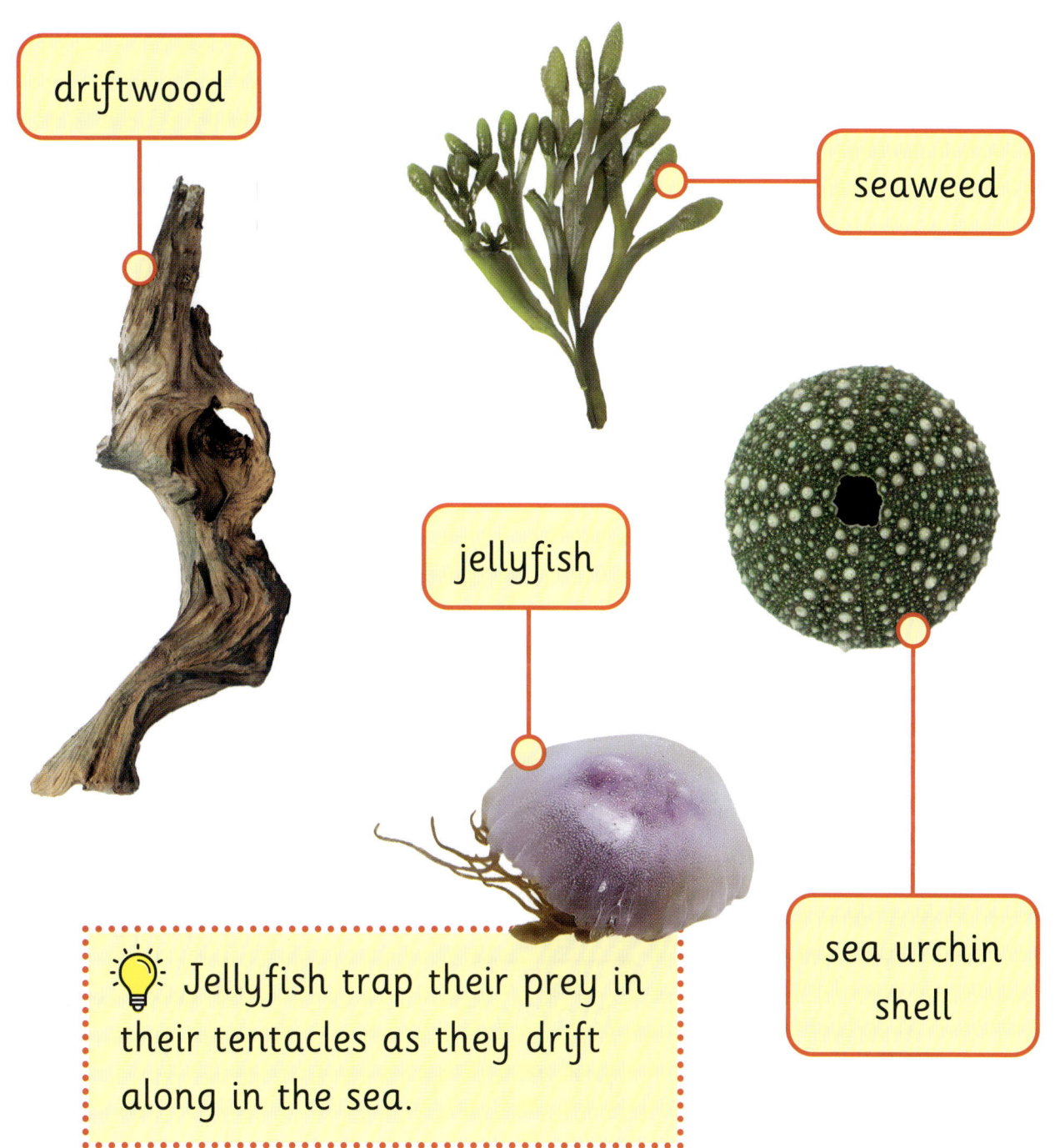

💡 Jellyfish trap their prey in their tentacles as they drift along in the sea.

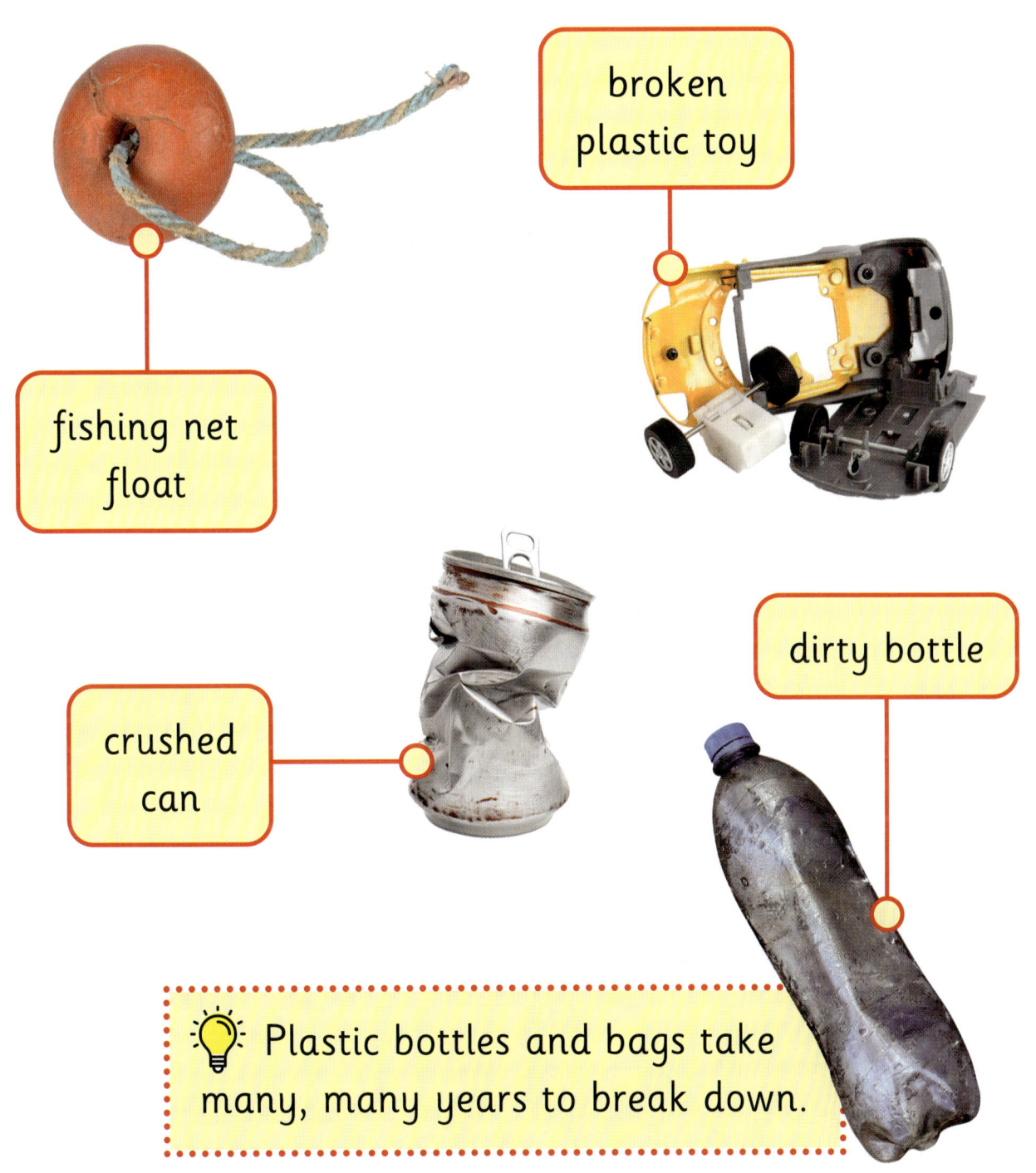

Rules for Beachcombing

You can keep some artificial finds, like sea glass and pottery. They are just very old litter! Some people make pretty things with them.

You should leave things from nature where they are. Some creatures hide and hunt in driftwood and seaweed. You should not spoil their homes.

You should not move or touch animals. This washed-up jellyfish cannot live out of water, but it can still sting you. Be cautious!

You should throw away some things. Pick up litter carefully and dispose of it properly.
This will stop it washing back into the water and harming animals. It will also keep our beaches clean for everyone.

Talk about it!